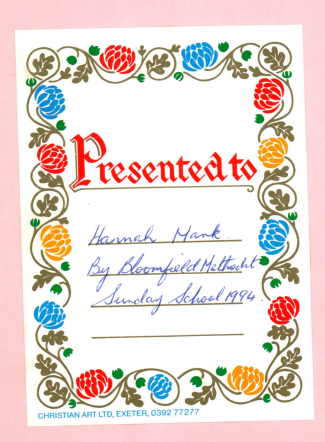

Presented to

Hannah Mark
By Bloomfield Methodist
Sunday School 1994

CHRISTIAN ART LTD, EXETER, 0392 77277

Noah's Story

Copyright © 1992 by Hunt & Thorpe
Text © Rhona Pipe
Illustrations © Jenny Press
Originally published by Hunt and Thorpe 1992
ISBN 1-85608-074-9

First published by Hunt & Thorpe 1992.
Published in Australia by Hunt & Thorpe Australia Pty Ltd,
9 Euston St, Rydalmere, NSW 2116.

The CIP catalogue record for this book is available from the British Library.

All rights reserved. Except for brief quotations in
critical articles or reviews, no part of this book may be
reproduced in any manner without prior permission from
the publishers. Write to: Hunt and Thorpe,
66 High St, Alton, Hants. GU34 1ET.

Manufactured in Singapore

Noah's Story

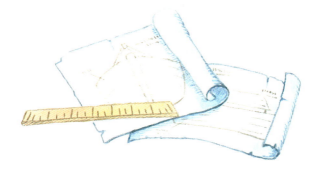

Rhona Pipe

Illustrated by
Jenny Press

Hunt & Thorpe

God was very sad.
The people he had made
had made up their minds
to hate him.
On top of that
They hated each other.
Only Noah was good.

God said to Noah,
'I'm going to put an end
to all these people.
Make a ship out of good timber.'
Noah began to cut down some trees,
and his three sons helped him.

God told Noah how to make the ship.
It was very big.
It had three decks,
and a roof,
and a lot of rooms.
All the people made fun of Noah.
'You're mad', they said.
'Where's the water?'

God said,
'Get 7 pairs of every kind of
"clean" animal
and 1 pair of every kind of
"unclean" animal
and take them on the boat.
Get plenty of food.'
And Noah did what God said.
'Now what's that madman up to?'
asked the people.

Noah went into the ship
with his wife, his sons
and their wives.
And God shut the door.
Then the wind came up.
It blew clouds across the sky.
Drops of rain began to fall.
But Noah was safe.

The rain fell.
It made pools on the ground.
The pools became a lake,
the lake became a sea.
And the ship drifted on the sea.
Soon there was only
the grey sea, under the grey sky
and the falling rain.
For 40 days the rain fell.

But God did not forget Noah.
One day, the rain stopped.
After a long time
the water began to go down
very slowly.
And the boat got stuck on a mountain.
Noah sent out a raven.
He never saw it again.

Then Noah sent out a dove.
There was nowhere for it to rest
so it came back.
After 7 days he sent it out again.
All day he waited.

In the evening, there was the dove
with a leaf in its beak.
At last the flood had gone!

One more week Noah waited
and then sent out the dove again.
She found a home on land
and did not come back.
So Noah took off the roof
and looked out.
Thick mud everywhere —
it was wonderful.

God said,
'You can all get out now.'
God put a rainbow in the sky.
He said: 'This rainbow is my promise
to you that I will never again
kill all the people in the world.'
And Noah and his family praised God.